Great Works

Instructional Guides
for Literature

The Day the Crayons Quit

A guide for the book by Drew Daywalt
Great Works Author: Jodene Lynn Smith, M.A.

Publishing Credits

Corinne Burton, M.A.Ed., *President*; Emily R. Smith, M.A.Ed., *Content Director*; Lee Aucoin, *Multimedia Designer*; Stephanie Bernard, *Assistant Editor*; Don Tran, *Production Artist*; Amber Goff, *Editorial Assistant*

Image Credits

Timothy J. Bradley (cover; pages 10–12, 22, 40, 46, 51, 60–62)

Standards

© 2007 Teachers of English to Speakers of Other Languages, Inc. (TESOL)
© 2007 Board of Regents of the University of Wisconsin System. World-Class Instructional Design and Assessment (WIDA)
© Copyright 2010. National Governors Association Center for Best Practices and Council of Chief State School Officers. All rights reserved.

Shell Education

5301 Oceanus Drive
Huntington Beach, CA 92649-1030
http://www.shelleducation.com
ISBN 978-1-4807-8506-9
© 2015 Shell Educational Publishing, Inc.

Table of contents

How to Use This Literature Guide

Today's standards demand rigor and relevance in the reading of complex texts. The units in this series guide teachers in a rich and deep exploration of worthwhile works of literature for classroom study. The most rigorous instruction can also be interesting and engaging!

Many current strategies for effective literacy instruction have been incorporated into these instructional guides for literature. Throughout the units, text-dependent questions are used to determine comprehension of the book as well as student interpretation of the vocabulary words. The books chosen for the series are complex and are exemplars of carefully crafted works of literature. Close reading is used throughout the units to guide students toward revisiting the text and using textual evidence to respond to prompts orally and in writing. Students must analyze the story elements in multiple assignments for each section of the book. All of these strategies work together to rigorously guide students through their study of literature.

The next few pages describe how to use this guide for a purposeful and meaningful literature study. Each section of this guide is set up in the same way to make it easier for you to implement the instruction in your classroom.

Theme Thoughts

The great works of literature used throughout this series have important themes that have been relevant to people for many years. Many of the themes will be discussed during the various sections of this instructional guide. However, it would also benefit students to have independent time to think about the key themes of the book.

Before students begin reading, have them complete the *Pre-Reading Theme Thoughts* (page 13). This graphic organizer will allow students to think about the themes outside the context of the story. They'll have the opportunity to evaluate statements based on important themes and defend their opinions. Be sure to keep students' papers for comparison to the *Post-Reading Theme Thoughts* (page 59). This graphic organizer is similar to the pre-reading activity. However, this time, students will be answering the questions from the point of view of one of the characters in the book. They have to think about how the character would feel about each statement and defend their thoughts. To conclude the activity, have students compare what they thought about the themes before they read the book to what the characters discovered during the story.

How to Use This Literature Guide (cont.)

Vocabulary

Each teacher reference vocabulary overview page has definitions and sentences about how key vocabulary words are used in the section. These words should be introduced and discussed with students. Students will use these words in different activities throughout the book.

On some of the vocabulary student pages, students are asked to answer text-related questions about vocabulary words from the sections. The following question stems will help you create your own vocabulary questions if you'd like to extend the discussion.

- How does this word describe _____'s character?
- How does this word connect to the problem in this story?
- How does this word help you understand the setting?
- Tell me how this word connects to the main idea of this story.
- What visual pictures does this word bring to your mind?
- Why do you think the author used this word?

At times, you may find that more work with the words will help students understand their meanings and importance. These quick vocabulary activities are a good way to further study the words.

- Students can play vocabulary concentration. Make one set of cards that has the words on them and another set with the definitions. Then, have students lay them out on the table and play concentration. The goal of the game is to match vocabulary words with their definitions. For early readers or English language learners, the two sets of cards could be the words and pictures of the words.

- Students can create word journal entries about the words. Students choose words they think are important and then describe why they think each word is important within the book. Early readers or English language learners could instead draw pictures about the words in a journal.

- Students can create puppets and use them to act out the vocabulary words from the stories. Students may also enjoy telling their own character-driven stories using vocabulary words from the original stories.

How to Use This Literature Guide (cont.)

Analyzing the Literature

After you have read each section with students, hold a small-group or whole-class discussion. Provided on the teacher reference page for each section are leveled questions. The questions are written at two levels of complexity to allow you to decide which questions best meet the needs of your students. The Level 1 questions are typically less abstract than the Level 2 questions. These questions are focused on the various story elements, such as character, setting, and plot. Be sure to add further questions as your students discuss what they've read. For each question, a few key points are provided for your reference as you discuss the book with students.

Reader Response

In today's classrooms, there are often great readers who are below average writers. So much time and energy is spent in classrooms getting students to read on grade level that little time is left to focus on writing skills. To help teachers include more writing in their daily literacy instruction, each section of this guide has a literature-based reader response prompt. Each of the three genres of writing is used in the reader responses within this guide: narrative, informative/explanatory, and opinion. Before students write, you may want to allow them time to draw pictures related to the topic. Book-themed writing paper is provided on page 69 if your students need more space to write.

Guided Close Reading

Within each section of this guide, it is suggested that you closely reread a portion of the text with your students. The sections to be reread are described by location within the story since there are no page numbers in these books. After rereading the section, there are a few text-dependent questions to be answered by students.

Working space has been provided to help students prepare for the group discussion. They should record their thoughts and ideas on the activity page and refer to it during your discussion. Rather than just taking notes, you may want to require students to write complete responses to the questions before discussing them with you.

Encourage students to read one question at a time and then go back to the text and discover the answer. Work with students to ensure that they use the text to determine their answers rather than making unsupported inferences. Suggested answers are provided in the answer key.

How to Use This Literature Guide (cont.)

Guided Close Reading (cont.)

The generic open-ended stems below can be used to write your own text-dependent questions if you would like to give students more practice.

- What words in the story support . . . ?
- What text helps you understand . . . ?
- Use the book to tell why _____ happens.
- Based on the events in the story, . . . ?
- Show me the part in the text that supports . . . .
- Use the text to tell why . . . .

Making Connections

The activities in this section help students make cross-curricular connections to mathematics, science, social studies, fine arts, or other curricular areas. These activities require higher-order thinking skills from students but also allow for creative thinking.

Language Learning

A special section has been set aside to connect the literature to language conventions. Through these activities, students will have opportunities to practice the conventions of standard English grammar, usage, capitalization, and punctuation.

Story Elements

It is important to spend time discussing what the common story elements are in literature. Understanding the characters, setting, plot, and theme can increase students' comprehension and appreciation of the story. If teachers begin discussing these elements in early childhood, students will more likely internalize the concepts and look for the elements in their independent reading. Another very important reason for focusing on the story elements is that students will be better writers if they think about how the stories they read are constructed.

In the story elements activities, students are asked to create work related to the characters, setting, or plot. Consider having students complete only one of these activities. If you give students a choice on this assignment, each student can decide to complete the activity that most appeals to him or her. Different intelligences are used so that the activities are diverse and interesting to all students.

How to Use This Literature Guide (cont.)

Culminating Activity

At the end of this instructional guide is a creative culminating activity that allows students the opportunity to share what they've learned from reading the book. This activity is open ended so that students can push themselves to create their own great works within your language arts classroom.

Comprehension Assessment

The questions in this section require students to think about the book they've read as well as the words that were used in the book. Some questions are tied to quotations from the book to engage students and require them to think about the text as they answer the questions.

Response to Literature

Finally, students are asked to respond to the literature by drawing pictures and writing about the characters and stories. A suggested rubric is provided for teacher reference.

Correlation to the Standards

Shell Education is committed to producing educational materials that are research and standards based. As part of this effort, we have correlated all of our products to the academic standards of all 50 states, the District of Columbia, the Department of Defense Dependents Schools, and all Canadian provinces.

Purpose and Intent of Standards

Standards are designed to focus instruction and guide adoption of curricula. Standards are statements that describe the criteria necessary for students to meet specific academic goals. They define the knowledge, skills, and content students should acquire at each level. Standards are also used to develop standardized tests to evaluate students' academic progress. Teachers are required to demonstrate how their lessons meet standards. Standards are used in the development of all of our products, so educators can be assured they meet high academic standards.

How to Find Standards Correlations

To print a customized correlation report of this product for your state, visit our website at http://www.shelleducation.com and follow the online directions. If you require assistance in printing correlation reports, please contact our Customer Service Department at 1-877-777-3450.

correlation to the standards (cont.)

standards correlation chart

The lessons in this book were written to support today's college and career readiness standards. The following chart indicates which lessons address each standards.

College and Career Readiness Standard	Section
Read closely to determine what the text says explicitly and to make logical inferences from it; cite specific textual evidence when writing or speaking to support conclusions drawn from the text. (R.1)	Guided Close Reading Sections 1–5; Analyzing the Literature Sections 1–5; Story Elements Sections 1–5
Determine central ideas or themes of a text and analyze their development; summarize the key supporting details and ideas. (R.2)	Analyzing the Literature Sections 1–5; Post-Reading Theme Thoughts; Culminating Activity
Analyze how and why individuals, events, or ideas develop and interact over the course of a text. (R.3)	Analyzing the Literature Sections 1–5; Guided Close Reading Sections 1–5; Story Elements Sections 1–5
Interpret words and phrases as they are used in a text, including determining technical, connotative, and figurative meanings, and analyze how specific word choices shape meaning or tone. (R.4)	Vocabulary Sections 1–5
Read and comprehend complex literary and informational texts independently and proficiently. (R.10)	Entire Unit
Write arguments to support claims in an analysis of substantive topics or texts using valid reasoning and relevant and sufficient evidence. (W.1)	Reader Response Sections 1, 4
Write informative/explanatory texts to examine and convey complex ideas and information clearly and accurately through the effective selection, organization, and analysis of content. (W.2)	Reader Response Section 2
Write narratives to develop real or imagined experiences or events using effective technique, well-chosen details and well-structured event sequences. (W.3)	Reader Response Sections 3, 5
Demonstrate command of the conventions of standard English grammar and usage when writing or speaking. (L.1)	Analyzing the Literature Sections 1–5; Language Learning Sections 1–5
Demonstrate command of the conventions of standard English capitalization, punctuation, and spelling when writing. (L.2)	Reader Response Sections 1–5; Language Learning Sections 1–3

correlation to the Standards (cont.)

Standards correlation chart (cont.)

College and Career Readiness Standard	Section
Demonstrate understanding of figurative language, word relationships, and nuances in word meanings. (L.5)	Vocabulary Sections 1–5; Language Learning Section 4
Acquire and use accurately a range of general academic and domain-specific words and phrases sufficient for reading, writing, speaking, and listening at the college and career readiness level; demonstrate independence in gathering vocabulary knowledge when encountering and unknown term important to comprehension or expression. (L.6)	Vocabulary Sections 1–5; Language Learning Section 4

TESOL and WIDA Standards

The lessons in this book promote English language development for English language learners. The following TESOL and WIDA English Language Development Standards are addressed through the activities in this book:

- **Standard 1:** English language learners communicate for social and instructional purposes within the school setting.

- **Standard 2:** English language learners communicate information, ideas and concepts necessary for academic success in the content area of language arts.

About the Author—Drew Daywalt

Although this is Drew Daywalt's debut book, he has been a writer for a long time. He graduated from Emerson College in Boston, Massachusetts, with a double major in screen writing and children's literature. Daywalt's career began as a writer and director in film and television. He wrote for MTV and Disney, including shows such as *Timon and Pumba*, *Buzz Lightyear of Star Command*, and *The Wacky World of Tex Avery*.

After much success in Hollywood, he decided to try writing a children's book. He got the idea for *The Day the Crayons Quit* while brainstorming ideas for books. He was staring at a box of crayons that had some colors used more than others, and the peach crayon had the wrapper torn off. The story *The Day the Crayons Quit* is a result of that moment.

Daywalt lives in Los Angeles with his wife, two kids, and a dog. He is working on a second book about the crayons and is doing research to write a new novel aimed at middle schoolers.

Possible Texts for Text Comparisons

The Day the Crayons Quit is Drew Daywalt's first book; however, there are a variety of themes and texts that this book can be used with for comparisons.

This text uses a series of letters to carry the storyline. An excellent series to use as a letter-writing text comparison is the I Wanna . . . series by Karen Kaufman Orloff (*I Wanna Iguana*, *I Wanna New Room*, and *I Wanna Go Home*).

The crayons in the story do not get along and each has reasons to quit. Books such as *How Do Dinosaurs Play with Their Friends?* by Jane Yolen can be used to draw students' attention to getting along, friendship, and reconciling differences.

Duncan, the boy to whom the letters are written, ends up using the crayons to create a picture with items colored in nontraditional colors. Explore the theme of creativity with books such as *A Day With No Crayons* by Elizabeth Rusch or *Beautiful Oops!* by Barney Saltzberg.

Finally, each crayon is a character with its own voice in *The Day the Crayons Quit*. Compare the crayons with characters that are each a letter of the alphabet in *Once Upon an Alphabet* by Oliver Jeffers.

Book Summary of *The Day the Crayons Quit*

Imagine his surprise when Duncan goes to take out his crayons and finds a stack of letters instead! Each letter has been written by one of his crayons and explains why it has quit.

Red feels it works too hard—even on holidays! White complains it cannot be seen when used on white paper. Yellow and orange both contend that they are the rightful color of the sun. The letters take the reader through twelve crayon colors from the box and their rationale for quitting.

After reading all of the letters, Duncan comes up with the perfect piece of art that has a solution to each crayon's complaint. Duncan's teacher likes his coloring and especially the creativity he shows in the solution!

Cross-Curricular Connection

This text can be used in a unit on the study of art and creativity.

Possible Texts for Text Sets

- Ahlberg, Allan. *The Pencil*. Candlewick, 2012.
- Johnson, Crockett. *Harold and the Purple Crayon*. HarperCollins, 2005.
- Reynolds, Peter H. *Sky Color*. Candlewick, 2012.
- Rickerty, Simon. *The Crayon: A Colorful Tale About Friendship*. Aladdin, 2014.
- Rusch, Elizabeth. *A Day with No Crayons*. Cooper Square Publishing, 2007.
- Saltzberg, Barney. *Beautiful Oops!* Workman Publishing Company, 2010.
- Saltzberg, Barney. *A Little Bit of Oomph!* Workman Publishing Company, 2013.

or

- Forman, Michael. *From Wax to Crayon*. Children's Press, 1997.
- Gibson, Ray. *What Shall I Draw*? Usborne Publishing Limited, 2002.
- Heller, Ruth. *Color*. Grosset & Dunlap, 1995.
- Peot, Margaret. *Inkblot*. Boyds Mills Press, 2011.
- Watt, Fiona. *The Usborne Book of Art Ideas*. Usborne Books, 2000.

Pre-Reading Theme Thoughts

Directions: Draw a picture of a happy face or a sad face. Your face should show how you feel about each statement. Then, use words to say what you think about each statement.

Statement	How Do You Feel? ☺ ☹	Why do You Feel This Way?
Crayons have feelings.		
Rainbows can be black.		
Others are affected when friends fight with each other.		
Pink is a girls' color.		

Vocabulary Overview

Key words and phrases from this book are provided below with definitions and sentences about how the words are used in the story. Introduce and discuss these important vocabulary words with students. If you think these words or other words in the story warrant more time devoted to them, there are suggestions in the introduction for other vocabulary activities (page 5).

Word	Definition	Sentence about Text
stack (opening page)	a neat pile of items	There are twelve letters in the **stack**.
rest (red page)	a break from working	Red Crayon needs to **rest**.
overworked (red page)	worked too much or too hard	Red Crayon is **overworked** because it colors for two holidays.
wizard (purple page)	a magical person	The **wizard's** hat is colored purple.
gorgeous (purple page)	very beautiful	Purple is a **gorgeous** color.
neither (beige page)	not one or the other	Beige Crayon is **neither** light brown nor dark brown.
proud (beige page)	having proper self-respect	Beige Crayon is **proud** to be its own color.
wheat (beige page)	a cereal grain that is often made into flour	The **wheat** growing in the field is beige.
honest (beige page)	truthful	Beige Crayon is **honest** in saying nobody likes to use it.
excited (beige page)	enthusiastic; eager	Kids are **excited** to use other color crayons, but not beige.

Vocabulary Activity

Directions: Draw a picture to illustrate each vocabulary phrase.

a child is **excited** for a holiday	a **gorgeous** dragon
a **wizard resting**	**wheat** that is **neither** tall nor yellow

Analyzing the Literature

Provided below are discussion questions you can use in small groups, with the whole class, or for written assignments. Each question is written at two levels so that you can choose the right question for each group of students. For each question, a few key points are provided for your reference as you discuss the book with students.

Story Element	Level 1	Level 2	Key Discussion Points
Plot	Where does Duncan find the letters?	Describe how Duncan finds the letters.	Duncan is in class and goes to get his crayons from their box when he finds the letters.
Plot	Why does Red Crayon need a rest?	What evidence is there that Red Crayon needs a rest?	Red Crayon says it has to work harder than all of the other crayons. It has to work all year long, even on holidays like Valentine's Day and Christmas.
Character	What word does Purple Crayon use to describe itself?	Describe Purple Crayon's character.	Purple Crayon describes itself as gorgeous. It is very neat and it does not want to be wasted by being used to color outside the lines.
Setting	What makes the illustration of the dragon so messy?	How do the illustrations support Purple Crayon's desire to be neat?	The illustration shows the purple being colored outside the lines on the dragon, the wizard's hat, and the wizard's clothes. Purple Crayon does not want to be wasted by coloring outside the lines.
Character	Why is Beige Crayon upset with Brown Crayon?	Why does Beige Crayon want to be called "beige"?	Beige Crayon feels as if Brown Crayon gets used more often. It wants to be called "beige" because it is not light brown nor dark tan. It is its own color.

Name _____

Reader Response

Think

Red Crayon is used for a lot of coloring. It has to work on holidays, too. Red Crayon thinks it is overworked. Think about whether Red Crayon needs a rest.

Opinion Writing Prompt

Write your opinion about whether or not Red Crayon needs a rest. Include at least one reason for your opinion.

_____
_ _
_____
_ _
_____
_ _
_____
_ _
_____
_ _
_____

Name _____

Guided close Reading

Closely reread the Beige Crayon page.

Directions: Think about these questions. In the space below, write ideas or draw pictures as you think. Be ready to share your answers.

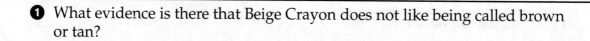

❶ What evidence is there that Beige Crayon does not like being called brown or tan?

❷ What does Beige Crayon think is unfair?

❸ Why doesn't Beige Crayon like to be used to color wheat?

Making connections—Holidays

Directions: Red Crayon complains that it is used to color Santa at Christmas and all the hearts at Valentine's Day. Fill in the chart below with the colors and symbols you associate with each holiday. There can be more than one color or symbol for each holiday.

Holidays	Colors	Symbols
Christmas	red, green, white	Santa, candy canes
Fourth of July		
Halloween		
Thanksgiving		
Hanukkah		
Valentine's Day		

Directions: Write a sentence to describe your favorite holiday.

_____

_ _ _ _ _ _ _ _ _ _ _

_____

_____

_ _ _ _ _ _ _ _ _ _ _

_____

Name _____

Language Learning—Commas

Directions: Commas are used to separate items in a list. Write a sentence listing the words in each box.

Example

grapes	dragons	wizards' hats

Purple Crayon is used for grapes, dragons, and wizards' hats.

1.

fire engines	apples	strawberries

_____

_ _ _ _ _ _ _ _ _ _ _ _ _ _ _ _ _ _

_____

_ _ _ _ _ _ _ _ _ _ _ _ _ _ _ _ _ _

2.

bears	ponies	puppies

_____

_ _ _ _ _ _ _ _ _ _ _ _ _ _ _ _ _ _

_____

_ _ _ _ _ _ _ _ _ _ _ _ _ _ _ _ _ _

3.

apples	bananas	peaches

_____

_ _ _ _ _ _ _ _ _ _ _ _ _ _ _ _ _ _

_____

_ _ _ _ _ _ _ _ _ _ _ _ _ _ _ _ _ _

Name _____

Story Elements—Character

Directions: Draw a line to match the crayon color with its characteristic.

purple
beige
red

overworked
neat
not used

Directions: Color the crayons below using purple, red, and beige.

Name _____

Story Elements—Setting

Directions: Red Crayon is used a lot at Christmas. Think about other things you see at Christmas. Draw a picture showing a Christmas setting. Be sure to use colors other than red!

Vocabulary Overview

Key words and phrases from this section are provided below with definitions and sentences about how the words are used in the story. Introduce and discuss these important vocabulary words with the students. If you think these words or other words in the story warrant more time devoted to them, there are suggestions in the introduction for other vocabulary activities (page 5).

Word	Definition	Sentence about Text
rhinos (gray page)	short term for rhinoceroses; animals that live in Africa or Asia with thick skin and horns	**Rhinos** are colored by Gray Crayon.
hippos (gray page)	short term for hippopotamuses; animals that live in Africa with large heads and short legs	Gray Crayon is used to color **hippos**, too.
humpback whales (gray page)	large whales that have curved backs and long flippers	Pictures of **humpback whales** make Gray Crayon tired.
penguins (gray page)	black and white birds that cannot fly and live in Antarctica	Gray Crayon points out that baby **penguins** are gray.
tiny (gray page)	very small	There are many **tiny** gray rocks.
pebbles (gray page)	small, round stones usually found in or near water	Gray Crayon is used to color rocks and **pebbles**.
page (white page)	a piece of paper	White Crayon cannot be seen when used on a white **page**.
outline (white page)	a line that marks the outer part of a shape	A black **outline** of a shape helps you know what is colored white.
empty (white page)	containing nothing	White Crayon feels **empty** because it cannot be seen well.
brighter (black page)	more clear or vivid in color	Every color is **brighter** than Black Crayon.

Name _____

Vocabulary Activity

Directions: Use the clues to complete the puzzle. Use the Word Bank to help.

Word Bank

outline	brighter	empty
tiny	hippo	page

Across

1 a line that marks the outer part of a shape

2 a piece of paper

3 very small

Down

4 short for hippopotamus

5 more clear or vivid in color

6 containing nothing

#40015—*Instructional Guide: The Day the Crayons Quit* © Shell Education

Analyzing the Literature

Provided here are discussion questions you can use in small groups, with the whole class, or for written assignments. Each question is written at two levels so that you can choose the right question for each group of students. For each question, a few key points are provided for your reference as you discuss the book with the students.

Story Element	Level 1	Level 2	Key Discussion Points
Character	What word does Gray Crayon use to describe itself?	Why does Gray Crayon describe itself as *tired*?	Gray Crayon describes itself as tired because it is used to color so many large things.
Setting	Describe the illustrations on the Gray Crayon page.	Why are the illustrations of the penguin and pebbles so small?	The illustrations that show the elephant, rhino, and hippo are drawn large so they take up a whole page of the book because they are large animals. The baby penguin and pebbles are drawn much smaller to show that gray can be used for small things, too.
Setting	Describe the illustration *White Cat in the Snow*.	How does the illustration *White Cat in the Snow* support White Crayon's letter?	*White Cat in the Snow* shows the eyes, nose, and whiskers of a cat, but the body cannot be seen. In its letter, White Crayon complains that white is the same color as the page and cannot be seen unless there is a black outline. The illustration shows the cat blending into the page because there is no outline.
Plot	What does Black Crayon want to be used to color?	Why does Black Crayon suggest coloring a black beach ball?	Black Crayon wants to be used to color a beach ball black. Beach balls are usually colored with many different colors, but Black Crayon wants to be used to color and not just to outline.

Name _____

Reader Response

Think

White Crayon is never used in a rainbow. Think about the colors used when drawing a rainbow.

Informative/Expository Writing Prompt

Draw a picture of a rainbow in the space below. Then, write about the colors you used and why.

_____

- - - - - - - - - - - - - - -

_____

- - - - - - - - - - - - - - -

_____

- - - - - - - - - - - - - - -

_____

- -

_____

- -

_____

- -

_____

Name _____

Guided close Reading

Closely reread the White Crayon page.

Directions: Think about these questions. In the space below, write ideas or draw pictures as you think. Be ready to share your answers.

❶ What does White Crayon complain it is used for?

❷ Why is Black Crayon needed as an outline to know white is on a page?

❸ What word is used to describe how White Crayon is feeling and why?

Name _____

Making connections—Animal colors

Directions: Gray Crayon is used for elephants, hippos, and rhinos. Complete the chart by listing animals for each color. Name more than one animal for each color if you can!

Color	Animals
gray	*elephants, rhinos, hippos, humpback whales, baby penguins*
red	
beige	
white	
black	
green	
yellow	
blue	
pink	

Name _____

Language Learning—Question Marks

Directions: Questions are easy to find in a text because they have question marks. Write a question that each crayon asks. Be sure to include a question mark at the end of each sentence.

Crayon	Question
Gray Crayon	
White Crayon	
Black Crayon	

Directions: Write your own question from White Crayon.

_____

_____

_____

_____

Name _____

Story Elements—Plot

Directions: Black Crayon wants to be used to color in some objects. In the left box, use a black crayon to draw and color a picture. Then, draw the same picture in the right box using any colors you want. Talk with a partner about which picture you like better and why.

Black Picture	Brighter Picture

Story Elements—Character

Directions: Choose one of the animals Gray Crayon has to color—an elephant, a rhino, a hippo, a humpback whale, or a baby penguin. Draw and color a picture of the animal.

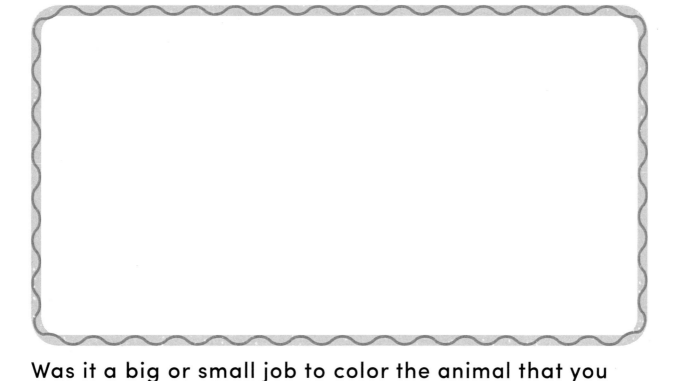

Was it a big or small job to color the animal that you chose? Why?

_____

_ _ _ _ _ _ _ _ _ _ _ _ _ _ _ _ _ _

_____

_ _ _ _ _ _ _ _ _ _ _ _ _ _ _ _ _ _

_____

_ _ _ _ _ _ _ _ _ _ _ _ _ _ _ _ _ _

_____

Vocabulary Overview

Key words and phrases from this section are provided below with definitions and sentences about how the words are used in the story. Introduce and discuss these important vocabulary words with the students. If you think these words or other words in the story warrant more time devoted to them, there are suggestions in the introduction for other vocabulary activities (page 5).

Word	Definition	Sentence about Text
congratulate (green page)	to wish joy	Green Crayon **congratulates** Duncan on his coloring.
career (green page)	a profession or job	Duncan's **career** of coloring things green has Green Crayon's approval.
settle (green page)	decide	Green Crayon wants to **settle** the fight between Yellow Crayon and Orange Crayon.
prove (yellow page)	to show the truth about something using evidence	Yellow Crayon wants to **prove** it is the color of the sun.
brilliantly (yellow page)	brightly	The sun shines **brilliantly** on the cornfield.
field (yellow page)	an open area of land	Duncan colors the **field** of corn yellow.
pal (yellow page)	a good or close friend	Yellow Crayon is a **pal** to Duncan.
true (yellow page)	agreeing with the facts	Yellow Crayon thinks yellow is the **true** color of the sun.
whiner (orange page)	a complainer	Orange Crayon says Yellow Crayon is a **whiner** for writing a letter to Duncan.
tattletale (orange page)	a person who tattles or tells the wrongs of another	Orange Crayon calls Yellow Crayon a **tattletale** for writing to Duncan.
clearly (orange page)	without question	Orange Crayon thinks orange is **clearly** the color of the sun.

Vocabulary Activity

Directions: Choose three vocabulary words from the list below. Write a sentence for each. Make sure your sentences show what the words mean.

Words from the Story

pal	field	congratulate
settle	true	prove

Word	Sentence

Directions: Answer this question.

1. What **career** would you like to have when you grow up?

_____

_ _ _ _ _ _ _ _ _ _ _ _ _ _ _ _ _ _ _ _

_____

Analyzing the Literature

Provided below are discussion questions you can use in small groups, with the whole class, or for written assignments. Each question is written at two levels so that you can choose the right question for each group of students. For each question, a few key points are provided for your reference as you discuss the book with students.

Story Element	Level 1	Level 2	Key Discussion Points
Setting	Which illustrations are shown on Green Crayon's page and also listed in the text? Which illustrations are not listed in the text?	How do the illustrations on Green Crayon's page support what its letter to Duncan says?	The illustrations that are also listed in the text include: a dinosaur, tree, frog, and crocodile. Not listed in the text, but shown in the illustrations, is a grasshopper. The page shows all these items colored with green because Green Crayon thinks Duncan is very successful when using green.
Plot	Why does Green Crayon write to Duncan?	Why is Green Crayon so concerned with the problem between Yellow Crayon and Orange Crayon?	Green Crayon wants to congratulate Duncan on his coloring career, and it wants to encourage Duncan to solve the problem between Yellow Crayon and Orange Crayon. Green Crayon wants the problem solved because Yellow Crayon and Orange Crayon are his friends, and their problem is driving everyone else crazy.
Plot	What is the problem between Yellow Crayon and Orange Crayon?	What reasons do Yellow Crayon and Orange Crayon give about why they should be the color of the sun?	Yellow Crayon and Orange Crayon both think they should be the color of the sun. Yellow Crayon reminds Duncan that it was used for the sun in a picture Duncan colored last Tuesday. Orange Crayon reminds Duncan that it was used for the sun in two pictures colored in a coloring book on Thursday.
Character	How does Orange Crayon describe Yellow Crayon?	What evidence is there that Yellow Crayon is a tattletale?	Orange Crayon describes Yellow Crayon as a "big whiner" and a tattletale. Yellow Crayon has already written to Duncan telling him that Orange Crayon and Yellow Crayon are not talking and trying to get Duncan to side with Yellow Crayon.

Reader Response

Think

Yellow Crayon and Orange Crayon are fighting. Think about a time you had a fight with someone.

Narrative Writing Prompt

Write about a time you had a fight with a friend. Write about what happened to cause the fight. Explain how you ended the fight.

_____

_____

_____

_____

_____

_____

_____

_____

_____

_____

_____

_____

_____

_____

_____

Guided Close Reading

Closely reread Green Crayon's page.

Directions: Think about these questions. In the space below, write ideas or draw pictures as you think. Be ready to share your answers.

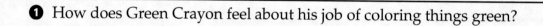

❶ How does Green Crayon feel about his job of coloring things green?

❷ How does Green Crayon feel about the fight between Yellow Crayon and Orange Crayon?

❸ What evidence is there that Green Crayon is not mad like the other crayons?

Making connections—Puns

Directions: Orange Crayon writes a pun in its letter. A **pun** is a play on words. The jokes below are puns. Circle the word or words that are being played with. Write the real meaning of the word that you circled.

Example: "(Orange) you glad I'm here?"

       Aren't

1. **Q:** What is a bee's favorite candy?

   A: Bumble gum

_____

- - - - - - - - - - - - - - - - - -

_____

2. **Q:** What did the egg say when he burped?

   A: Egg-scuse me!

_____

- - - - - - - - - - - - - - - - - -

_____

3. **Q:** Where does Batman take a shower?

   A: In the bat-room

_____

- - - - - - - - - - - - - - - - - -

_____

Name _____

Language Learning—contractions

Directions: Write the contractions for the words below. Then, circle the letters that are removed from the original words to make the contractions.

Word Bank

isn't	didn't	can't
we're	it's	don't

1. cannot _____

2. we are _____

3. it is _____

4. do not _____

5. did not _____

6. is not _____

Directions: Write a sentence using the contraction for *I am.*

_____

_____

_____

Story Elements—character

Directions: Reread the pages with Yellow Crayon and Orange Crayon. Think about what you can tell about each crayon's character from the illustrations and the text. Draw or write about what the illustrations and text tell you.

Yellow Crayon	Orange Crayon
What the illustration tells me	What the illustration tells me
What the text tells me	What the text tells me

Name _____

Story Elements—Plot

Directions: Both Yellow Crayon and Orange Crayon think they are the color of the sun. What are the reasons they each feel the way that they do? Then, write your opinion about which one is right.

Yellow Crayon's Reasons

_____

- -

_____

- -

_____

Orange Crayon's Reasons

_____

- -

_____

- -

_____

Your Opinion

_____

- -

_____

- -

_____

Vocabulary Overview

Key words and phrases from this section are provided below with definitions and sentences about how the words are used in the story. Introduce and discuss these important vocabulary words with the students. If you think these words or other words in the story warrant more time devoted to them, there are suggestions in the introduction for other vocabulary activities (page 5).

Word	Definition	Sentence about Text
stubby (blue page)	short and broad	Blue Crayon has been used so much it is **stubby**.
railing (blue page)	a barrier that supports	Blue Crayon cannot see over the **railing** of the crayon box.
once (pink page)	one time	Duncan has not even used Pink Crayon **once**.
fabulous (pink page)	very good	Duncan's sister does a **fabulous** job coloring inside the lines.
occasional (pink page)	sometimes	Pink Crayon thinks Duncan should use pink to color an **occasional** monster.
unused (pink page)	not been used before	Pink Crayon is **unused** by Duncan.
embarrassed (peach page)	self-conscious or distressed	Peach Crayon feels **embarrassed** to leave the box without its wrapper.
poor (conclusion)	worthy of pity or sympathy	**Poor** Duncan has to read all the letters.
idea (conclusion)	a plan of action	Duncan's **idea** is to draw a picture.
A+ (conclusion)	the highest grade that can be given	The teacher gives Duncan's picture the grade of **A+**.
creativity (conclusion)	the ability to create new and original things	Duncan's colorful picture shows **creativity**.

Name _____

Vocabulary Activity

Directions: Review the words and definitions. Then, answer the questions.

1. **once:** one time

   What is something you have only done **once**?

   _____
   - - - - - - - - - - - - - - - - -
   _____
   _____
   - - - - - - - - - - - - - - - - -
   _____

2. **occasional:** sometimes

   What is something you do **occasionally**?

   _____
   - - - - - - - - - - - - - - - - -
   _____
   _____
   - - - - - - - - - - - - - - - - -
   _____

3. **fabulous:** very good

   What are you **fabulous** at doing?

   _____
   - - - - - - - - - - - - - - - - -
   _____
   _____
   - - - - - - - - - - - - - - - - -
   _____

Analyzing the Literature

Provided below are discussion questions you can use in small groups, with the whole class, or for written assignments. Each question is written at two levels so that you can choose the right question for each group of students. For each question, a few key points are provided for your reference as you discuss the book with students.

Story Element	Level 1	Level 2	Key Discussion Points
Character	Describe how Blue Crayon looks.	Why does Blue Crayon look short and stubby?	Blue Crayon is described as short and stubby because Duncan uses it a lot and has for the past several years. Blue is Duncan's favorite color.
Plot	Why does Pink Crayon think Duncan has not used it?	Describe what Pink Crayon says about Duncan and his sister.	Pink Crayon thinks Duncan has not used it because it is a girls' color. Pink Crayon thinks Duncan's sister did a fabulous job coloring a princess with it.
Setting	Why is Peach Crayon shown inside the crayon box in the illustration?	How does the illustration of Peach Crayon support the text?	Peach Crayon is described in the text as being naked and too embarrassed to leave the box. The illustration shows Peach Crayon in the box with a distressed look on its face. The peach wrapper is on the ground next to the box.
Plot	Describe the final picture Duncan colors.	Explain why Duncan's picture is not colored using traditional colors.	The items in Duncan's picture are colored using non-traditional colors. For example, the rainbow is black, the dinosaur is pink, and the cowboy is pink. Each of the crayons had written Duncan a letter explaining why it quit. Duncan used the crayons in a non-traditional way in response to the crayons' letters.

Name _____

Reader Response

Think

Pink Crayon thinks Duncan has not used it because it is a girls' color. Think about whether you agree with that or not.

Opinion Writing Prompt

Write your opinion about whether or not pink is a girls' color. Include at least one reason for your opinion.

_____

_____

_____

_____

_____

_____

_____

_____

_____

_____

_____

Guided close Reading

| Closely reread Pink Crayon's page. | **Directions:** Think about these questions. In the space below, write ideas or draw pictures as you think. Be ready to share your answers. |

❶ What words does Pink Crayon use that show it feels upset and left out?

❷ Why does Pink Crayon think Duncan has not used it?

❸ How does Pink Crayon think it should be used?

Name _____

Making connections—Social Studies

Directions: Blue is used on maps to show water. Label each type of water shown below. Then, use your blue crayon to color the water. Use other crayon colors to color the areas surrounding the water.

Word Bank

pond	river	ocean	lake

1.

_____

- - - - - - - - - - - - - - - - -

_____

a large body of salt water

2.

_____

- - - - - - - - - - - - - - - - -

_____

a natural stream of water that flows

3.

_____

- - - - - - - - - - - - - - - - -

_____

a large body of standing water

4.

_____

- - - - - - - - - - - - - - - - -

_____

a body of water smaller than a lake

Language Learning—
Shades of Meaning

Directions: Below are words that can be used to describe how well something is done. Write the words in order on the lines below.

Word Bank

terrible	good
bad	amazing

Best

_____

_ _ _ _ _ _ _ _ _ _ _ _

_____

_____

_ _ _ _ _ _ _ _ _ _ _ _

_____

_ _ _ _ _ _ _ _ _ _ _ _

_____

_____

_ _ _ _ _ _ _ _ _ _ _ _

_____

Worst

Name _____

Story Elements—Character

Directions: Each crayon closes its letter with a description of itself. Answer each question below.

Why does Blue Crayon say it's stubby?	
Why does Pink Crayon say it's unused?	
Why does Peach Crayon say it's naked?	

Story Elements—Setting

Directions: Pink Crayon wants to be used. Draw a picture below showing a dinosaur, monster, or cowboy. Be sure to color the character pink! Then, write a sentence describing the setting you drew.

_____

_____

_____

_____

Book Overview

Lessons in this section are included for an additional piece of literature. *The Crayon Box that Talked* by Shane DeRolf tells the story of crayons that are fighting because each thinks it is the best color. A little girl overhears the crayons and buys them. She uses the crayons to create a beautiful picture in which each of them is used. This piece of literature and the corresponding lesson provide students with an opportunity to compare and contrast *The Day the Crayons Quit*. Both pieces of literature include crayons as main characters, but more than that, both approach the idea of creativity from a different angle.

Vocabulary Overview

Key words and phrases from this section are provided below with definitions and sentences about how the words are used in the story. Introduce and discuss these important vocabulary words with the students. If you think these words or other words in the story warrant more time devoted to them, there are suggestions in the introduction for other vocabulary activities (page 5).

Word	Definition	Sentence about Text
overheard	heard what was said without the speaker knowing	The girl **overhears** the crayons talking.
laid	put down	The girl has **laid** out all the crayons on her bed.
drifting	moving along by water, wind, or air	White clouds are **drifting** in the sky.
terrific	very good	Blue looks **terrific** as the color of the sky.
unique	one of a kind	Each crayon color is **unique**.
complete	having all the right parts	When the colors come together, the picture is **complete**.

Name _____

Vocabulary Activity

Directions: Draw a line from each vocabulary word to the picture that best shows the word in use.

overheard

laid

drifting

terrific

Directions: Write a sentence using either the word **complete** or **unique**.

_____

_ _

_____

_ _

_____

Analyzing the Literature

Provided below are discussion questions you can use in small groups, with the whole class, or for written assignments. Each question is written at two levels so that you can choose the right question for each group of students. For each question, a few key points are provided for your reference as you discuss the book with students.

Story Element	Level 1	Level 2	Key Discussion Points
Plot	How does the girl find out about the crayons' fight?	How does the illustration help show the girl overhearing the crayons fighting?	The girl overhears the crayons fighting in the store. The illustration shows the crayons fighting in the background and the girl with her hand to her ear as if she is listening to what is happening.
Plot	Where does the girl put the crayons when she gets home?	What is the importance of the girl laying out the crayons on her bed?	The girl lays out the crayons on her bed. She does this so the crayons can watch as she colors the picture. She wants them to realize that each color is important to completing the picture.
Setting	Describe the setting of the picture the girl draws.	Describe the crayons' reaction to the picture the girl draws.	The girl draws an outdoor scene which requires her to use all of the colors from the crayon box. The crayons are shown in the foreground smiling and giving each other high fives, because they realize they are each important to the picture.
Character	Describe the crayons at the beginning of the book. Describe the crayons at the end of the book.	What causes the crayons' attitudes to change from the beginning of the book to the end of the book?	At the beginning of the book, the crayons are upset with each other. After seeing the girl's picture, they understand that each is important to creating a completed picture. At the end of the book, the crayons are complimenting each other and realize that they are each unique.

Reader Response

Think

The crayons do not get along at first but are friends later. Think about a time you did not get along with someone and how you made up.

Narrative Writing Prompt

Write about a time you did not get along with someone and how you made up.

_____

_____

_____

_____

_____

_____

_____

_____

_____

_____

_____

_____

Name _____

Guided close Reading

Closely reread from where the crayons talk to each other about the girl's drawing to the end of the book.

Directions: Think about these questions. In the space below, write ideas or draw pictures as you think. Be ready to share your answers.

❶ In what way is blue used in the picture?

❷ How does the illustration support the word **unique** that is used in the text?

❸ What makes the picture complete?

Name _____

Making connections—Making color

Directions: Answer the color combination questions. Then, color in the labeled circles. For the sections that overlap, use your answers to help choose the right colors.

1. What color is made when yellow and blue combine?

_____

_____

2. What color is made when red and yellow combine?

_____

_____

3. What color is made when red and blue combine?

_____

_____

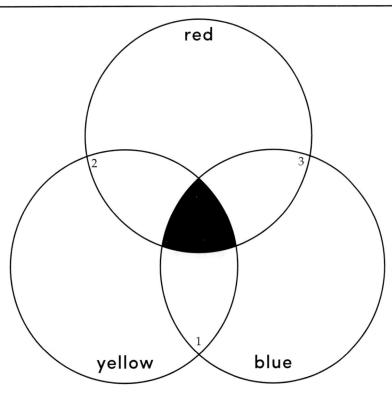

Name _____

Language Learning—Verbs

Directions: Fill in the endings of the verbs below.

Root Verb	-s	-ed
1. **talk**	talks	talked
2. **walk**		
3. **like**		
4. **color**		
5. **drift**		

 #40015—Instructional Guide: The Day the Crayons Quit

Story Elements—Setting

Directions: The setting of this story changes. Illustrate both settings of the book.

1st Setting

2nd Setting

Name _____

Story Elements—Plot

Directions: In the top chart, write what each crayon is upset about at the beginning of the book. Then, in the bottom chart, write what each crayon says at the end of the book.

Beginning of Book

Yellow	
Green	

End of Book

Yellow	
Green	

Name _____

Post-Reading Theme Thoughts

Directions: Choose a main character from *The Day the Crayons Quit.* Pretend you are that character. Draw a picture of a happy face or a sad face to show how the character would feel about each statement. Then, use words to explain your picture.

Character I Chose: _____

Statement	How Do You Feel? 😊 ☹	Explain Your Answer
Crayons have feelings.		
Rainbows can be black.		
Others are affected when friends fight with each other.		
Pink is a girls' color.		

Culminating Activity: Retelling and Extending the Story

Directions: Reproduce the crayon picture cards on pages 61–62 on tagboard or construction paper. Have students color the pieces and cut them out along the dashed lines.

Follow the sequence below to practice retelling the story.

1. Emphasize with students the following attributes of a good retelling:
   - Include the names of the characters.
   - Include the setting.
   - Include the events that happen in the correct sequence.

2. Model for students a good retelling of the story. Use the crayon picture cards as you retell the story so students can see how the picture cards help you remember the characters and the sequence of events.

3. Place students with partners. Assist students in lining up their picture cards in the order they will use them when retelling the story.

4. Have students practice retelling the story to their partners. Encourage students to help each other remember all of the events in the sequence of the retelling. If needed, assist students in writing one or two words on the back of each crayon picture card that will help them remember why the crayon quit. For example, on the back of the yellow and orange crayons, students can write the word *sun*. This should be enough to help students remember that the orange and yellow crayons both thought they were the real color of the sun.

5. Once students have a firm understanding of the story, have them create their own crayon character using a color that is not in *The Day the Crayons Quit*. Students can create their own character using the pattern on this page. Then, copy and provide students with the letter template on page 63. Have students write letters from the crayons they created. The letters should explain why they quit.

culminating Activity: Retelling
and Extending the Story *(cont.)*

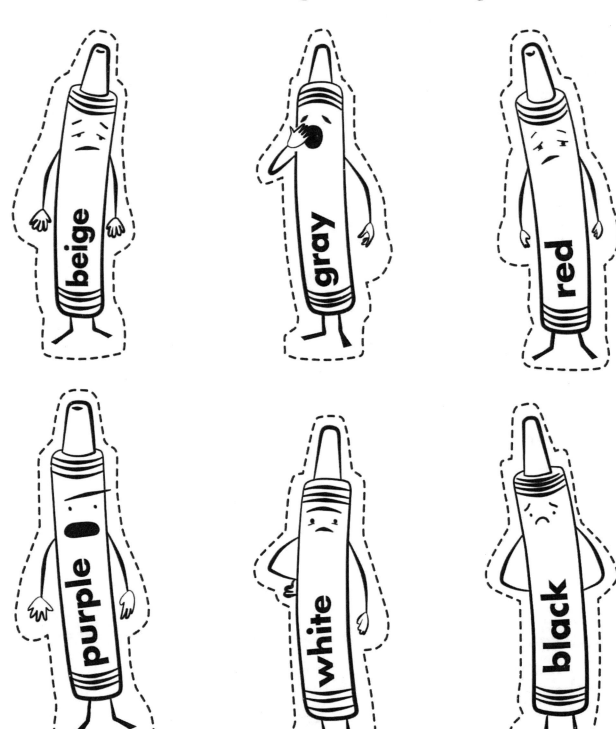

Culminating Activity: Retelling and Extending the Story *(cont.)*

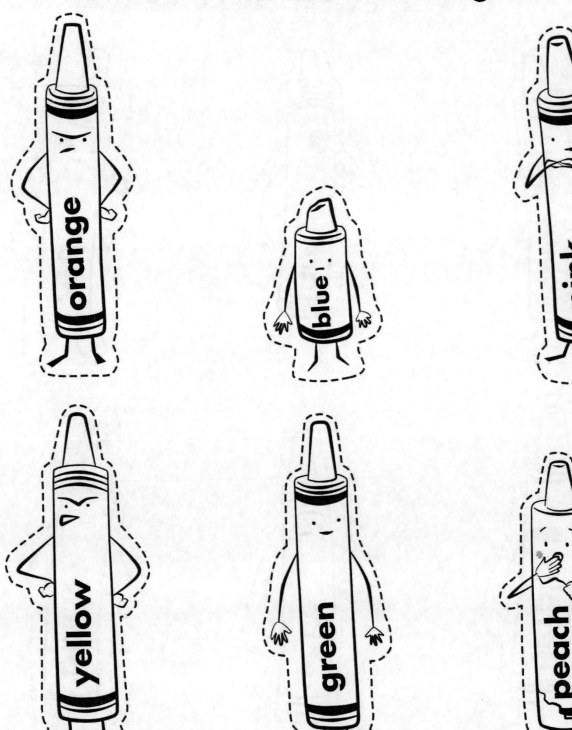

Culminating Activity: Retelling and Extending the Story (cont.)

Dear Duncan,

_____

— — — — — — — — — — — — — — — —

_____

_____

— — — — — — — — — — — — — — — —

_____

_____

— — — — — — — — — — — — — — — —

_____

_____

— — — — — — — — — — — — — — — —

_____

From,

_____

— — — — — — — — — — — — — — — —

_____

Name _____

comprehension Assessment

Directions: Fill in the bubble for the best response to each question.

Section 1: Beginning-Beige Crayon
1. What is Red Crayon's complaint?

    (A) It has to work on holidays.

    (B) It is used so much that it is now stubby.

    (C) It needs a break.

    (D) It cannot be seen.

Section 2: Gray Crayon-Black Crayon
2. Why can't White Crayon be seen?

    (A) Duncan does not use it.

    (B) It is the same color as the page.

    (C) It has a black outline.

    (D) It is on black paper.

Section 3: Green Crayon-Yellow Crayon
3. What is one reason Green Crayon writes its letter?

    (A) It is never used.

    (B) It is used to color frogs.

    (C) It thinks it is being used too much.

    (D) Its friends are fighting and it wants Duncan to help.

comprehension Assessment *(cont.)*

Section 4: Blue crayon-End of Book

4. Describe the things that Pink Crayon thinks Duncan should use it to color.

_____

_____

_____

_____

_____

_____

_____

_____

_____

_____

Section 5: The crayon Box that Talked

5. What do the crayons realize when they see the girl's picture?

    Ⓐ The girl uses markers to make her picture.

    Ⓑ Each crayon is needed to make the picture.

    Ⓒ Red crayon is the only color needed.

    Ⓓ The girl likes blue crayon the best.

Name _____

Response to Literature: Traditional versus creative

Directions: Using a pencil, draw two identical pictures. Then, color the first picture using traditional colors for each item. Use nontraditional colors and your creativity to color the second picture.

Traditional Picture

Creative Picture

Name _____

Response to Literature:
Traditional versus creative *(cont.)*

Directions: Answer the questions below about the traditional and creative pictures you drew.

1. Describe one item in your traditional picture. Which color did you choose to use?

   _____

   _____

   _____

   _____

   _____

2. Describe which nontraditional color you chose for an item in your creative picture and why.

   _____

   _____

   _____

   _____

   _____

3. Which picture do you like better? Why?

   _____

   _____

   _____

   _____

   _____

Name _____

Response to Literature Rubric

Directions: Use this rubric to evaluate student responses.

Great Job	Good Work	Keep Trying
☐ You answered all three questions completely. You included many details.	☐ You answered all three questions.	☐ You did not answer all three questions.
☐ Your handwriting is very neat. There are no spelling errors.	☐ Your handwriting can be neater. There are some spelling errors.	☐ Your handwriting is not very neat. There are many spelling errors.
☐ Your pictures are neat and fully colored.	☐ Your pictures are neat and some of them are colored.	☐ Your pictures are not very neat and/or fully colored.
☐ Creativity is clear in the pictures and the writing.	☐ Creativity is clear in either the pictures or the writing.	☐ There is not much creativity in either the pictures or the writing.

Teacher Comments: _____

_____

_____

_____

Name _____

The responses provided here are just examples of what students may answer. Many accurate responses are possible for the questions throughout this unit.

Vocabulary Activity—Section 1: Beginning–Beige Crayon (page 15)

Pictures will vary. Check for illustrations that include depictions of the italicized vocabulary words.

Guided Close Reading Activity—Section 1: Beginning–Beige Crayon (page 18)

1. Beige Crayon says it is tired of being called light brown or dark tan and taking second place to Brown Crayon. It is proud of being beige.

2. Beige Crayon does not think it is fair that Brown Crayon gets to color all the bears, ponies, and puppies. Beige Crayon only gets to color turkey dinner and wheat.

3. Kids don't get excited about coloring wheat.

Making Connections—Section 1: Beginning–Beige Crayon (page 19)

Students' answers will vary. Suggested answers are provided below.

Holidays	Colors	Symbols
Christmas	red, green, white	Santa, candy canes
Fourth of July	red, white, and blue	flags, Uncle Sam
Halloween	orange, black	pumpkins, skeletons, witches
Thanksgiving	brown, orange	turkeys, pilgrims
Hanukkah	blue, white	menorahs, dreidels
Valentine's Day	pink, red, and white	hearts, Cupid

Sentences will vary. Check that students' sentences include their favorite holidays.

Language Learning—Section 1: Beginning–Beige Crayon (page 20)

Sentences will vary. Check for commas used correctly in the series.

1. Red Crayon is used for fire engines, apples, and strawberries.

2. Brown Crayon is used for bears, ponies, and puppies.

3. My favorite fruits are apples, bananas, and peaches.

Story Elements—Section 1: Beginning–Beige Crayon (page 21)

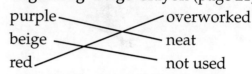

purple — overworked
beige — neat
red — not used

Vocabulary Activity—Section 2: Gray Crayon–Black Crayon (page 24)

Across
1. outline
2. page
3. tiny

Down
4. hippo
5. brighter
6. empty

Guided Close Reading—Section 2: Gray Crayon–Black Crayon (page 27)

1. White complains it is only used to color snow or fill in empty space between other things.

2. Paper is also white, so you cannot see white crayon on white paper. Black Crayon is needed to outline.

3. White Crayon is feeling empty because it is only used to fill in empty spaces.

Language Learning—Section 2:
Gray Crayon–Black Crayon (page 29)

Crayon	Question
Gray Crayon*	"How about one of those once in a while to give me a break?"
White Crayon	"You color with me, but why?"
Black Crayon*	"How about a black beach ball sometime?"

*Gray Crayon and Black Crayon each ask more than one question. Check to make sure the questions asked are for the correct crayons.

Guided Close Reading—Section 3:
Green Crayon–Yellow Crayon (page 36)

1. Green Crayon likes its job of coloring loads of "crocodiles, trees, dinosaurs, and frogs."
2. Green Crayon is friends with both Yellow Crayon and Orange Crayon, and he is asking for Duncan's help in settling the fight because they are driving Green Crayon crazy.
3. Green Crayon signs its letter from "your happy friend."

Making Connections—Section 3:
Green Crayon–Yellow Crayon (page 37)

1. (Bumble)gum   bubble
2. (egg-scuse) me   excuse
3. (bat-room)   bathroom

Language Learning—Section 3:
Green Crayon–Yellow Crayon (page 38)

1. can(not)   can't
2. we (a)re   we're
3. it (i)s   it's
4. do n(o)t   don't
5. did n(o)t   didn't
6. is n(o)t   isn't

Story Elements—Section 3:
Green Crayon–Yellow Crayon (page 39)

- **Yellow Crayon**—Yellow Crayon tries to convince Duncan that it is right. It uses the word *brilliantly* to describe itself in the picture of the sun and corn.
- **Orange Crayon**—Orange Crayon tries to convince Duncan that it is right. It calls Yellow Crayon a big whiner and a tattletale. Orange Crayon is funny because it uses a pun to make a joke in its letter.

Story Elements—Section 3:
Green Crayon–Yellow Crayon (page 40)

- Yellow Crayon's Reasons—Yellow Crayon's reason is that Duncan used it to color the sun and the cornfield in a picture.
- Orange Crayon's Reasons—Orange Crayon's reason is that Duncan used it to color the sun in two pictures.

Guided Close Reading—Section 4:
Blue Crayon–End of Book (page 45)

1. Pink Crayon uses the word *unused*.
2. Pink Crayon thinks Duncan thinks that pink is a girls' color.
3. Pink Crayon thinks it should be used for dinosaurs, monsters, and cowboys.

Making Connections—Section 4:
Blue Crayon–End of Book (page 46)

1. ocean   2. river
3. lake   4. pond

Language Learning—Section 4:
Blue Crayon–End of Book (page 47)

Best
amazing
good
bad
terrible
Worst

Story Elements—Section 4:
Blue Crayon–End of Book (page 48)

Blue Crayon stubby	Blue Crayon has been used to color a lot this past year so it is short.
Pink Crayon unused	Pink Crayon has not been used by Duncan one time in the past year.
Peach Crayon naked	Peach Crayon's wrapper is not on it.

Vocabulary Activity—Section 5:
The Crayon Box That Talked (page 51)

- overheard—child with hand up to ear
- laid—child laying a book and crayons on the bed
- drifting—child floating on an inner tube
- terrific—school paper with an A+ on it

Guided Close Reading—Section 5:
The Crayon Box That Talked (page 54)

1. Blue is used for the sky.
2. Each crayon is needed to color something different in the picture, so each is uniquely used.
3. The picture is complete because each crayon colored a part of the picture.

Making Connections—Section 5
The Crayon Box That Talked (page 55)

1. green
2. orange
3. purple

Language Learning—Section 5:
The Crayon Box That Talked (page 56)

Root Verb	-s	-ed
1. **talk**	talks	talked
2. **walk**	walks	walked
3. **like**	likes	liked
4. **color**	colors	colored
5. **drift**	drifts	drifted

Story Elements—Section 5:
The Crayon Box That Talked (page 58)
Beginning of Book

Yellow	"I don't like Red!"
Green	". . . Nor do I! And no one here likes Orange, but no one knows just why."

End of Book

Yellow	"I do like Red!"
Green	". . . So do I! And, Blue, you were terrific, so high up in the sky!"

Comprehension Assessment (page 64)

1. A. It has to work on holidays.
2. B. It is the same color as the page.
3. D. Its friends are fighting and it wants Duncan to help.
4. Pink Crayon thinks that Duncan should use it to color dinosaurs, monsters, and cowboys.
5. B. Each crayon is needed to make the picture.